50 Bedtime Stories To Inspire Girls

by

Lisa Hill

Stories to inspire you ....

Research by Alun Hill

Words by Lisa Hill and Colleen Damon

Graphics by Vlada Repeykova

Lady Diana

Diana, Princess of Wales was the first wife to Prince Charles of Wales.

She supported many charities, and was considered a great role model for young ladies.

She was born on 1 July, 1961 in Norfolk, and she was one of five children.

Her family had always been connected to the British Royal Family.

Her grandmothers helped assist the Queen's Mother, and some of Lady Diana's family were Royals too!

Lady Diana met Prince Charles as a young woman.

They were very popular together – their wedding was even watched by millions of people across the world.

They had two children together: Princes William and Harry.

Many people praised Lady Diana's style, but her most important work was in charity where she helped anybody in need.

Sadly, Lady Diana died in a car crash in 1997 while the media were chasing after her.

Her kind heart and actions are still remembered by the world today.

Indira Gandhi

Indira Gandhi is to this day the only woman to be Prime Minister of India.

She was born on 19 November 1917, in Allahabad, an only child to India's first Prime Minister.

She was known to be a firm leader and sent India to war while she ruled.

As a young child she as very unhappy, because her father was often away on business, and her mother was usually sick before she died.

She studied at Oxford University, and did well in history, economics and political studies.

Indira Gandhi met her husband while she was studying in Europe, and they had two children together.

Although many people disagreed with the way she ruled the country, she was also praised for helping India become independently run and making great developments in agriculture.

She was tragically shot and assassinated by two of her bodyguards on 31 October 1984.

The great role she played in India's history is still honoured today.

Indira Ghandi

Queen Victoria

Queen Victoria was born on 24 May 1819 at Kensington Palace, London.

Her father Edward was a Duke, and her mother Victoria was Princess of Germany.

Her royal upbringing was a protected one.

She did not play much with other children and was mainly surrounded by her adult teachers.

She was very artistic and enjoyed writing as she got older.

She became Queen of the United Kingdom when she was 18 year old.

She strived to be a good Queen, and even paid off her father's debt.

She was popular with her people from the beginning of her rule.

She married the German Prince Albert in 1839 and they had nine children together!

Great Britain did very well under her rule, as industries expanded and it was a time of peace.

She was also known as the Empress of India.

Queen Victoria died on 22 January 1901 at the age of 81, after a very prosperous rule.

Queen Victoria

Benazir Bhutto

Benazir Bhutto was the Prime Minister of Pakistan twice.

She was born on 21 June 1953, in Karachi, Pakistan.

She was the first woman to be elected in a democratic vote in a Muslim Country.

She was the eldest of four children, and grew up speaking both English and Urdu.

She was a good student and completed degrees in the USA, including a degree from Harvard.

She loved her life as a student, and said her college years were some of her happiest.

She married her husband in 1987 and they had three children together.

She became the first woman to have a baby while working in government office in recent times.

Benazir was very famous, and people admired that she was such a strong leader and helped revolutionised women's rights.

Benazir died on 27 December 2007 after being shot.

The United Nations, and many female activists all over the world, are still angered by her death.

Benazir Bhutto

Jackie Kennedy

Jacqueline Kennedy Onassis was born on 28 July 1929.

She was wife to United States President John F. Kennedy.

As a young lady she got a degree in French literature, and worked at a newspaper as a photographer.

Later in her life she also worked as a book editor.

A year after college Jacky met the President at a dinner party.

They were married a year later and the couple had four children.

Jacky was very greatly admired for her beauty and intelligence.

She was with her husband, the President, when he was assassinated in 1963.

She then married her second husband, the Greek shipping Magnate Aristotle Onassis.

Jacky died 19 May 1994, after a struggle with cancer.

She is remembered as an intelligent and graceful woman.

People considered her to be a fashion icon, and praised her for her elegance and charm.

She remains one of the most popular First Ladies of America.

JACQUELINE
KENNEDY ONASSIS

Cleopatra

Cleopatra was an Egyptian Princess.

She was born 69 BC.

She was the last Pharaoh (Egyptian Royal leader) of Ancient Egypt.

Growing up she was extremely clever, and her father's favorite child.

She learnt a lot from her father, the Pharaoh, about how the country was ruled.

She grew up speaking and writing Greek, and also knew Egyptian and Italian, among many other languages.

Cleopatra and her brother were married so that they could rule over Egypt together.

She became the one ruler of Egypt after her brother died.

The country did very well under Cleopatra's rule, and her people loved her.

She met the Roman leader, Marc Antony, in 41 BC and the two fell in love.

They even fought war together!

Cleopatra died after hearing that Marc Antony had died.

She allowed a venomous cobra to bite her.

There are still many stories regarding Cleopatra's beauty and intelligence.

CLEOPATRA

Joan of Arc

Joan of Arc was a French military leader, leading the French in a war against England at a very young age.

Joan of Arc was born in a small town in France in 1412.

From a young age Joan had visions from God that told her to lead the army.

Joan decided to follow her visions at the age of 16.

Joan received helped from King Charles of France.

He listened to her visions and put her in the army.

She became very good at horse riding and fighting.

She helped the army win a battle against the English in Orleans.

Joan was captured by the English in a battle in Compiegne.

The English put Joan on trial and accused her of being a witch.

They could not find any evidence of witchcraft, so they put her to death for dressing like a man. Joan was burnt alive at 19 years old.

Thankfully the church honored Joan by making her a Saint.

Joan of Arc

Marilyn Monroe

Marilyn Monroe was a beautiful American actress and model.

She was born Norma Jeane Mortenson on 01 June 1926.

Her childhood was not a particularly happy one.

To escape this, she married her neighbor's son shortly after turning 16.

The marriage did not last.

It was one of three marriages during her lifetime.

Marilyn changed her look when she started becoming interested in modelling and became an actress.

Although her early films were not successful, she soon gained popularity.

She was known for playing a typical "silly" blonde girl.

Marilyn was also known to use her attractiveness to gain work and attention.

She is most well-known for singing happy birthday to President John F. Kennedy at Madison Square Garden in New York.

Most people think they had a secret relationship.

Marilyn died 5 August 1962 after a drug overdose, at 36 years old.

She is still considered a modern female icon of beauty.

Marilyn Monroe

Mother Teresa

Mother Teresa was a well-respected, and much loved humanitarian.

She was born 26 August 1910, in the Ottoman Empire.

She was raised Roman Catholic, and she made the decision to devote her life to God when she was still very young.

At 18, she took steps toward becoming a missionary.

She learnt English, and a started her missionary work in India a year later. She became a teacher and even learnt the local language.

God spoke to her at the age of 36 to help the poor in India.

It was a difficult task: she had no support and often went hungry herself while trying to help the poor!

Eventually she gained support and started the Missionaries of Charity organisation.

Mother Teresa gained recognition as the true humanitarian she was, and helped countless many sick, impoverished and malnourished people.

She died 5 September 1997 after her health started failing.

She is also known as Blessed Teresa of Calcutta.

Mother Teresa

Anne Frank

Anne Frank was a young victim of the Holocaust, and is most famous for the diary she left behind.

Anne was born on 12 June 1929 in Frankfurt, Germany.

She was a very confident and vibrant young girl.

She had an older sister and many friends.

She dreamt of being a writer.

Her family were Jewish.

The rise of Adolf Hitler in 1933 caused many Jewish families to flee from Germany.

Hitler despised Jewish people, and their lives were in danger.

Anne's family moved to the Netherlands and lived a good life until World War II began.

Anne's father gave her a journal for her 13th birthday.

She wrote in her journal while her family was in hiding for nearly 2 years.

Her family was sadly captured and separated.

She died from Typhus in March 1945.

When Anne's father returned, he found her diary and published it.

It became very famous, and still touches people's hearts with her stories of the struggle during the Holocaust.

Anne Frank

Audrey Hepburn

Audrey Hepburn was an iconic, award – winning American Actress.

She was born 4 May 1929, to an Aristocratic Dutch family.

She had to change her name during World War II to protect herself and her mother.

She danced ballet to collect money, and she struggled during the famine.

When the war was over, she and her mother moved to London.

Audrey studied ballet, modelled and started acting.

Her acting talents were immediately recognized and she quickly rose to fame.

Many of her male co-workers admired her charm and beauty.

She was popular among people too. She was a kind and humble person.

Audrey starred in many iconic movies, including *My Fair Lady* and *Breakfast at Tiffany's.*

She married twice and also had two children.

Audrey was also a philanthropist who helped many people.

She died 20 January 1993 from cancer.

She remains an icon for her timeless beauty, style and kindness.

Oprah Winfrey

Oprah Winfrey was born on 29 January 1954 in Kosciusko, Mississippi.

She is a world famous actress, but is better known for hosting her own TV show, The Oprah Winfrey Show.

Oprah's mother meant to name her Orpah, a name from the Bible, but she misspelled it to Oprah.

Oprah learnt to read and write from the Bible when she was very young.

Oprah's childhood was a difficult one.

She moved around a lot with her mother, and despite this and not having money, she did well at school.

Oprah did work in radio before she started doing the news on TV.

Oprah then hosted a talk show and knew that that was what she loved.

She started the Oprah Winfrey Show and it became very successful.

The show was on TV for 25 years.

Oprah helped many people through her show.

She now has her own TV network called the Oprah Winfrey Network.

Oprah Winfrey

Billie Jean King

Billie Jean King is a tennis champion and an activist for equality.

She was born on 22 November 1943 in Long Beach, California.

She learnt to play tennis on the public courts growing up.

Her younger brother is also a famous sports star.

Billie Jean is a record – holder, having won hundreds of titles in tennis.

Billie Jean also helped the world of tennis by exposing corruption and breaking limitations against women in sport.

Billie Jean was married to a famous lawyer involved in tennis, Larry King, but they later divorced.

She is an activist in women's rights, and often works for charities that support women in sport.

She also participated in many events that teach people about a healthy and fit lifestyle.

Billie Jean was the first President of the Women's Tennis Players Union.

She has received many awards and honors in her career, and for her charity work.

She now lives with her partner in both New York and Chicago.

Eleanor of Aquitaine

Eleanor of Aquitaine was a Duchess of the French region Aquitaine, born in 1122.

She was a very powerful and rich woman for her time.

She was married to two Kings during her life!

First she was married to King Louis VII, then she was married to King Henry II.

She was a smart, educated lady, learning about maritime laws and introducing them into her own lands.

She took part in the Crusades (wars), and was criticized for going against society with her strong attitudes.

Eleanor had 2 daughters with King Louis and eight children with King Henry!

She was thrown into prison by her husband, King Henry, because she supported their son's attack on his rule.

When King Henry died, Eleanor's son Richard became King and she helped him rule once more.

Eleanor lived a long life, dying in 1204.

She is buried with her husband, King Henry, and her son, Richard.

Eleanor of Aquitaine

Brigitte Bardot

Brigitte Bardot was born on 28 September 1934, in Paris.

She is a famous French actress, model, singer and animal rights activist.

Brigitte first trained as a ballerina when she was younger, before she started to model and act.

Originally, Brigitte appeared mainly in French films, doing very few English movies.

She was however very popular in America, and she soon became an international sensation because of her successful movies and her beauty.

She received a lot of attention when she wore a bikini in a movie in the 1950s!

These days Brigitte is much more famous for her work in animal rights.

She started the Brigitte Bardot Foundation in 1986, which protects the wellbeing of animals.

She is a vegetarian and protects many endangered animals with her donations and activism.

Brigitte has had four husbands during her lifetime, and one son.

She is now over 80 years old and still appears in the news with her activism, and strong political views.

Brigitte Bardot

Eleanor Roosevelt

Eleanor Roosevelt was the First Lady of the United States of America.

Her husband was President Franklin D. Roosevelt.

She was well known as a diplomat and activist.

She was born on 11 October 1884 in New York, to a prominent family.

Her uncle, Theodore Roosevelt, was President of the United States too.

However, her childhood was not a particularly happy one as she lost both her parents at a young age, and did not have many friends.

As Eleanor grew older, her confidence grew.

She had many well–known friends, including Amelia Earhart.

She married her husband on 17 March 1905.

They had six children together.

Eleanor was a strong and powerful voice for the rights of African Americans.

She voiced these views at a time when this was not common.

She even invited many African – Americans as guests to the White House!

She died on 7 November 1962 from heart failure.

She is said to have the first monument honoring a First Lady.

Eleanor Roosevelt

Coco Chanel

Coco Chanel was a famous French fashion designer.

She was born Gabrielle Chanel on 19 August 1883 in France.

She was one of five children.

Her father travelled often and her mother died when she was very young.

The family did not have a lot of money, and Coco spent time in an orphanage.

Although Coco could sew from the age of six, she did not have the money for her designs.

As a young and beautiful lady, Coco had the attention of wealthy men, and one of them – Captain Arthur Edward Capel – helped Coco with the money to open her first fashion shops.

Coco was revolutionary as a fashion designer.

She invented the "little black dress", reinvented woman's fashion and popularized costume jewelry.

She is maybe most well known for her wonderful Chanel perfumes.

She died on 10 January 1971, at the age of 87.

Her classic sense of style and perfumes are still famous and popular today.

Coco Chanel

Margaret Thatcher

Margaret Thatcher was the first female Prime Minister of the United Kingdom.

She was born on the 13 October 1925, in England.

She was nicknamed The Iron Lady, due to her strong leadership style.

Growing up, Margaret was a bright and clever student.

She did very well in school; and her hobbies included sports, poetry and piano.

She learnt about politics from her father, but she studied Chemistry at university.

She obtained a degree from Oxford.

Margaret entered politics some years after university.

She was a strong willed lady with powerful ideas, and she became Prime Minister on 4 May 1979.

She played a significant role in the UK war victories, and helped improve the economy of the United Kingdom.

She was a very strong leader, and retired from parliament in 1992.

Margaret was married to her husband Denis, until his death.

They had two children together.

She died on 8 April 2013 after suffering a stroke.

She remains highly honored.

Margaret Thatcher

J.K. Rowling

Joanne Rowling is a very successful, famous writer.

She is most well-known for authoring the Harry Potter series, a story of a young wizard's battle against darkness.

These books have sold over 400 million copies!

She was born 31 July 1965 in England.

She always loved writing, and penned her first story about a rabbit at a very young age.

She obtained a degree in French and Classics, and a few years afterward she married and had a daughter.

Her marriage did not last, and she struggled to support herself and her daughter.

J.K. Rowling formed the story of Harry Potter while on a train one day, and started writing immediately when she got home.

Although the story did not become an immediate success, she did not give up.

Soon, the books began to sell out, and a series of movies were made based on her Harry Potter series.

Her story is truly one of rags to riches.

She has now remarried, and lives in Scotland.

She supports many charities.

J.K. Rowling

Queen Elizabeth I

Queen Elizabeth I was Queen of England.

She was born 7 September 1533 in England, daughter to Henry VIII and Queen Anne.

Sadly, her father sentenced her mother to death because she could not give him a baby boy.

The King remarried and had a son, Prince Edward, so Elizabeth was no longer heir to the throne.

Her father died when she was 13, and Edward became King.

When he died, her half-sister Mary became queen.

Mary was worried Elizabeth would try to take the throne, and so Elizabeth was jailed!

Elizabeth Finally became Queen when Mary died.

She was a good Queen, and ruled for 44 years!

England won a war against France under her rule, and the country prospered and expanded.

This period is known as the Elizabethan Age.

It is still considered to be a golden time in England's history.

She did not marry or have children.

Queen Elizabeth died 24 March 1609.

Elizabeth I

Angela Merkel

Angela Merkel is the Chancellor of Germany.

She was born 17 July 1954 in West Germany.

She is a former scientist.

She was born to an affluent family, and was raised in a religious home.

She was a top student in school, and was awarded for her skills in mathematics and her fluency in Russian.

She studied physics at university.

Her career in politics started in the early 90s.

She became Minister for Women and Youth, and Minister for the Environment and Nuclear Safety.

This helped her career greatly.

In November 2005 she became the Chancellor of Germany.

Angela Merkel is married to her second husband, and she has no children.

She says that she loves football, and often attends international matches to support Germany.

Angela has won many honors and awards as a powerful, influential leader.

She is well respected and liked by the people of her country, and the world.

Catherine the Great

Catherine the Great was an Empress of Russia.

She was the most praised female ruler of Russia, and the longest ruling.

She was born on 2 May 1729, in Prussia (an old region of Europe).

She was born a princess, but her family were not wealthy.

She met her husband when she was only 10 years old, but did not like him.

Catherine began ruling Russia after her husband, Peter III of Russia, was assassinated.

She became Empress in 1762 and ruled Russia until her death in 1796.

Catherine is remembered as a great leader.

She strongly believed in the education of her people.

Catherine wrote a novel for the education of children and founded a school.

She was a progressive leader, and Russia expanded under during her reign.

Catherine the Great died on 17 November 1796, after a very successful rule, from a stroke.

Her son Paul took the crown after her death.

Catherine the Great

Jane Austen

Jane Austen was a very popular and well – known English author.

Her stories were often romantic, but also focused on important issues of the time; such as the divisions of classes, and women's rights.

She was born on 16 December 1775.

Both she and her sister were educated at Oxford until their parents could not afford it any more.

Jane loved being in her father's library and he encouraged the children to write.

Jane's family was also very involved in the theatre when she was younger.

As an adult, Jane lived the life typical for women of the time, though she continued writing.

With her brother's help, she had one of her books, Sense and Sensibility, published.

It was a very successful and popular story, and Jane's writing career blossomed.

Jane did not marry, and did not have children.

She died 18 July 1817, after falling ill.

Her books are still studied and loved today.

Jane Austen

Harriet Beecher Stowe

Harriet Beecher Stowe was a famous American writer and activist against slavery.

Harriet published 30 books during her life.

Her most famous novel is a book depicting the cruelty of slavery.

Although many people supported her, many people disliked her strong anti–slavery opinions too.

She was born on 14 June 1811 in Connecticut, USA.

She was one of 13 children!

Some of her brothers and sisters were well – known public figures too.

She was a good student growing up.

She met her husband at a literary club. He too spoke out against slavery.

They had seven children together.

Harriet met President Lincoln in November 1862.

She and her daughter reported that the visit with the President was quite fun!

Harriet suffered from Alzheimer's before her death on 1 July 1896.

They are many monuments dedicated to Harriet Beecher Stowe, and many honors dedicated to her activism in ending slavery, and helping revolutionize human rights.

Harriet Beecher Stowe

Estee Lauder

Estee Lauder was a very successful business woman, known for her cosmetics empire.

She was born 1 July 1906 in New York, USA.

She and her other siblings would often work in her father's warehouse store, and it was here that she development business skills.

When Estee was older she agreed to help her uncle with his business, where he made lotions and other cosmetics.

Estee enjoyed it and learnt a lot.

She became more interested in her uncle's business than her father's!

Estee introduced her own fragrance in 1953 and it was very successful, selling 50 000 samples in one year!

From there, her career and her empire took off.

Estee met her husband and marred while in her early 20s.

The couple had 2 children together.

Estee died on 24 April 2004 at the age of 97.

Estee Lauder remains a successful and popular brand among modern women to this day.

Estee Lauder

Florence Nightingale

Florence Nightingale was a respected and famous nurse, also known as "The Lady with the Lamp".

She was born in Italy on 12 May 1820, to a wealthy father.

He was a progressive man, believing that all children should be educated.

He taught Florence and her sister many subjects.

From a young age she loved helping the sick, including the servants and even the pets!

She also believed that God had called her to help the sick.

Her father did not want her to be a nurse, because she had such a good education, but he eventually allowed her to study nursing in Germany.

Florence attended to many sick people, but she is especially remembered for helping soldiers during war.

Florence was a very dedicated, kind person, and everyone around her noticed.

She helped improved the conditions the sick and wounded soldiers were confined too: feeding them, and nursing them.

Florence showed that nursing is a noble profession.

She died in her sleep at age 90 on 13 August 1910.

Florence Nightingale

Susan B. Anthony

Susan B. Anthony was a well–respected civil rights leader.

She was born 15 February 1820, in the USA.

She fought to help women get the right to vote.

Susan had 6 brothers and sisters, some of whom were also activists.

She was home schooled.

Things became difficult when her father lost all his money because of the failing economy.

She started teaching to help her father pay debts.

Susan was a strong and intelligent woman who believed that men and women should have equal rights, and that women should also vote to decide on the country's President.

Susan would speak at conventions and even voted when it was illegal for her to do so!

She was fined for this, but never paid the fine and continued to fight for her beliefs.

Susan died 13 March 1906, and it would be another 14 years after her death until women could vote in the USA.

Susan Anthony

Emily Dickinson

Emily Dickinson was a famous American poet.

She wrote almost 1800 poems over her lifetime!

Emily was born on 10 December 1830 in America to a prominent family.

Emily was described as a good child, and she was well educated.

As she grew older and experienced death in her family, she became saddened but soon recovered.

Emily was a very proficient poet, and those who knew her knew that she loved to write, but they did not understand just how much.

Only around 12 poems that Emily had written were published during her life.

In the year 1858, Emily started compiling her poems in a book.

This book, along with her other works, was only discovered after her death.

Emily was not a very sociable person, and was very withdrawn from the public.

Emily did not marry or have children.

She died at the age of 55 on 15 May 1886.

She is considered to be one of America's most important poets.

Emily Dickinson

Emmeline Pankhurst

Emmeline Pankhurst was a British activist, fighting for the right for women to vote.

She was born on 15 July 1858 in England to parents that were both politically involved.

She was one of 11 children!

Emmeline loved reading.

Her parents did not believe in educating girls, though her parents did believe in a woman's right to vote, and this started her passion in fighting for liberation.

Emmeline met her husband, Richard Pankhurst, at the age of 20, and they had five children together.

He was a strong supporter of women's rights.

Emmeline loved entertaining many famous and important guests at their house.

Emmeline and the women that she protested with were known for being quite extreme and radical in fighting for women's rights.

This often led to trouble with the law. She also provided relief to the poor and hungry.

Her struggle had a positive outcome.

Women gained the right to vote shortly before Emmeline died on 14 June 1928.

Emmeline Pankhurst

Marie Curie

Marie Curie was a famous scientist, known for her achievements in the field of radioactivity.

Her work helped progress modern science.

She was born 7 November 1867 in Warsaw, Poland.

She was the youngest of five children, and her parents were both teachers.

She was a bright child, learning to read and write at a young age.

However, there was a series of deaths in her family, and her father lost his job because of politics in Poland.

Marie had to go to university in Paris, because women could not study in Poland at the time.

She knew she wanted to be a scientist, and obtained a degree in physics.

Her husband, Pierre Curie, was also a scientist.

They had two children.

Marie is most well known for her achievements in radioactivity and X – rays.

She was the first women to win the Nobel Prize, and she won it twice!

She and her husband also discovered new elements.

She died on 4 July 1934 from overexposure to radiation.

Marie Curie

Catherine de Medici

Catherine de Medici was an Italian Noblewoman who also ruled as the Queen of France.

She was born 13 April 1519 in Florence to a catholic family.

Sadly, she was orphaned at a young age and went to live with her grandmother, who raised her.

At the young age of only 14, she married Henry, son of King Francis of France.

Henry went on to become King of France, making Catherine de Medici the new Queen.

The couple had 10 children together!

Her husband, the King, did not allow Catherine any real power or authority as Queen.

It was only after his death that she assumed a role of power.

Three of Catherine's sons ruled as the King of France during her lifetime!

It is because of Catherine's guidance and advice to her sons that they were able to rule and remain in power.

Because of this, she is widely considered to be the most powerful woman in Europe of her time.

She died 5 January 1589 at the age of 69.

Catherine de Medici

Helen Keller

Helen Keller was an activist for the deaf and the blind.

She was born 27 June 1880 in the USA, and grew up on a farm in Alabama.

She lost her sight and hearing when she was only a year and a half, due to illness.

Her parents employed a specialist, Annie Sullivan, to help their daughter learn to read Braille.

Annie and Helen remained friends for 50 years!

Helen also learnt to talk from another specialist, Sarah Fuller.

Helen took all she had learnt and invested it into helping others who suffered from disabilities, doing charity and raising awareness.

She often wrote about her own experiences too.

Helen had many famous friends including the author, Mark Twain, and the inventor, Alexander Graham Bell.

Helen even met a few presidents during her lifetime!

She died 1 June 1968.

She is remembered for the great strides she took in her campaigns for the disabled.

Helen Keller

Emily Bronte

Emily Bronte was a famous English novelist and poet.

She was born 30 July 1818 in England.

Some of Emily's other siblings grew to be quite famous too.

Emily always enjoyed writing poetry.

She was sent to be educated at the same school as two of her sisters, but disease broke out at the school and the girls were forced to return home.

Her sisters sadly died as a result of this.

Despite not having any formal education after this event, Emily was still very literate and intelligent.

Emily had also been sick as a child.

Emily became a teacher at the age of twenty, and she continued to write her poetry.

However, the long teaching hours were tough.

Emily eventually had her most well–known work, Wuthering Heights, published.

She gained success and recognition for her works.

Unfortunately, she died 19 December 1848 at the young age of 30 – only one year after the book's publication.

Her writing is still very popular.

Emily Bronte

Amelia Earhart

Amelia Earhart was a famous pioneer in female aviation.

She was born 24 July 1817 in Kansas, USA.

Amelia and her sister loved being adventurous while growing up.

They enjoyed collecting insects and other bugs, and playing together.

Amelia even enjoyed shooting rodents in her father's barn with a .22 rifle!

Though Amelia always had a love and fascination for flight, she did not show much interest when she saw one of the first planes the Wright brothers were flying.

She went on to study and enter the field of medical research.

She flew for the first time at an air show that she attended with her father in 1920.

From then onwards she knew what her passion was.

Amelia was incredible and set many records; becoming the first woman to cross oceans while flying Solo!

She received many honors for her work.

Amelia disappeared while attempting a solo flight across the pacific on 2 July 1937, and was declared dead on 5 January 1939.

Raisa Gorbachev

Raisa Gorbachev was the first lady of the Soviet Union from 1988 to 1991.

She was born on 5 January 1932 in the Soviet Union and was the eldest of three children.

Her husband was the Soviet leader Mikhail Gorbachev, and together they had one daughter.

They met while they were both studying philosophy at university.

Raisa is known for the charity and causes that she cared so dearly for.

She was involved in raising funds for preserving Soviet cultural heritage, and she especially worked in charity for children with blood cancer.

Raisa was also very involved with outreaches for women, speaking at conventions to help encourage and motivate women.

Raisa became sick and was diagnosed with leukemia.

She died 20 September 1999 at the age of 67.

Her family started the Raisa Gorbachev Foundation, which raises money in support of children suffering from cancer.

This ensured that her legacy lives on.

Raisa Gorbachev

Katharine Hepburn

Katharine Hepburn was a famous American actress who was known for her wide variety of roles, and her very strong personality.

She was born 12 May 1907 in the USA to wealthy parents who encouraged her independent nature.

She was described as a tomboy growing up, and had always been a fan of the movies.

Her brother's death when she was a teen made her sad and moody.

Katharine started acting while she was in college, when she got into the theatre.

She was soon discovered by an agent and went on to star in very popular and successful movies.

Her career spanned over 60 years and she won four Academy Awards!

Katharine was known for not buying into the Hollywood life of a movie star, nor the typical life that society thought was proper for a woman.

She was strong willed and independent!

She died 29 June 2003 at the age of 96.

Katharine Hepburn

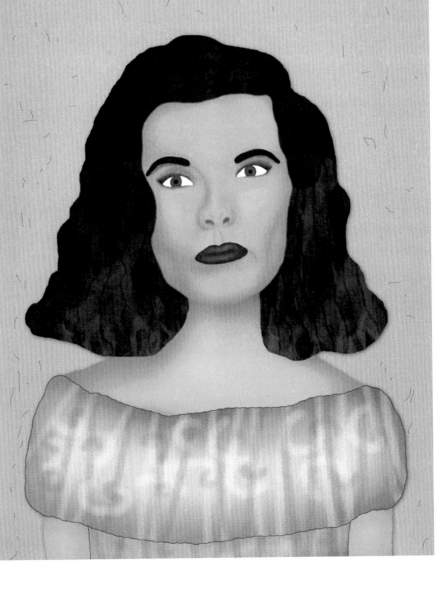

Billie Holiday

Billie Holiday was a world – renowned jazz singer and songwriter.

She was born on 7 April 1915 in the United States.

Billie Holiday's childhood was a very sad and difficult one.

Her father was absent and her mother was poor.

Billie Holiday found criminal ways in which to earn some kind of living, and because of this she spent time in jail.

She was even arrested at the young age of 14.

Billie started singing in nightclubs when she was a little older, as an alternative way to earn some money, and as a way to express herself.

These performances at the club led her to being signed for recording at the age of 18.

The songs did well and she became very successful.

Her career spanned over 30 years! She performed at Carnegie Hall and received many honors.

She had a powerful voice and is described as having an ongoing influence in music.

Sadly, Billie Holiday struggled with addiction.

She died 17 July 1959 at the age of 44.

Billie Holiday

Rosa Parks

Rosa Parks was a respected and famous civil rights activist.

She was born on 4 February 1913 in Alabama, USA, and is most well–known for the Montgomery Bus Boycott.

Rosa and her brother grew up on a farm with their grandparents.

She attended school but had to dropout to care for her ill mother.

A few years later, Rosa married and was able to complete her education.

Rosa and her husband wanted to fight against segregation in America.

When the Freedom Train (which opposed segregation too) came passed their town, Rosa led a group of people to join the movement.

While Rosa was on a bus home from work one day, she was asked to stand up for a white man and she refused.

The consequences of this was that large groups of African – Americans boycotted the bus service.

The boycotts lasted 381 days!

Eventually, thanks to Rosa, laws against segregation came into effect.

Rosa died on 24 October 2005.

Eva Peron

Eva Peron was an actress and the First Lady of Argentina, from 1946 until her death.

She was born on 7 May 1919 in Argentina.

She had a rural upbringing.

Though her father was a wealthy man, he had another family too.

He left Eva's family in poverty to return to his first family.

Eva always loved the cinema.

She moved away from her life in poverty to start acting and modelling.

She had success with the radio dramas that she did.

Eva met her husband, the soon to be Argentinian President, at a fundraiser.

Eva was involved in many charities and foundations during her time as first lady.

She helped the poor, and focused on empowering and encouraging women too. She also supported the cause for women to earn voting rights.

Her own foundation was very successful, and she helped many people through it.

Eva died from cancer at age 33 on 26 July 1952.

Eva Peron

Simone de Beauvoir

Simone de Beauvoir was a French writer, philosopher and activist, who was also involved in social issues and politics.

She was born 9 January 1908 in France, and her family struggled after World War 1.

Her father once described her as saying that she thinks like a man!

(Probably because she was so strong willed and intelligent!).

Simone studied mathematics and philosophy, and obtained a degree therein.

She was a very dedicated and intelligent student.

Simone had a lifelong relationship with another famous philosopher and novelist – Jean-Paul Sartre.

The couple did not have any children together.

Simone was involved in many causes socially and politically, but one of her main causes was the women's liberation movement.

Both Simone and her husband also wrote extensively on a wide variety of topics.

She is commonly regarded a fore founder of feminist philosophy, though she did not consider herself to be a philosopher.

She died from pneumonia on 14 April 1986.

Simone de Beauvoir

Germaine Greer

Germaine Greer is a well–known Australian writer, and an advocate for women's rights.

Germaine was born on 29 January 1939.

She is one of three children, and left home at the age of 18.

She obtained a degree in English and French language and literature.

Germaine has only been married once.

She was quite young and the marriage did not last long – only a few short weeks.

Germaine eventually started writing for an Australian magazine column.

She gained widespread attention because of this, and she moved on to writing books and appearing as a guest speaker.

She is very well known for her strong opinions and views on women's rights.

She is a very outspoken women!

Most of Germaine's writing focuses on feminism.

She said that she believes in the liberation of women more than she believes in equality.

She continues to write and voice her opinions.

GERMAINE GREER

Martina Navratilova

Martina Navratilova is a retired Czechoslovakian/ American tennis champion and tennis coach.

She was born 18 October 1956 in Czechoslovakia.

She is considered to be one of the greatest tennis players of all time, and she has earned many titles and honors, and has broken quite a few sports records too!

Martina started playing tennis from a very young age, and was exceptionally good at it.

She won her first professional title at only 17 years old!

Among some of Martina's accomplishments is that she was number one for 332 weeks in singles tennis, and she was also number one for 237 weeks in doubles tennis.

Martina also coached tennis for some time, and is known for some revolutionary techniques for training in tennis.

She is a breast cancer survivor.

Martina is involved in charities, and she mainly does work that involves caring for animals and children.

Martina Navratilova

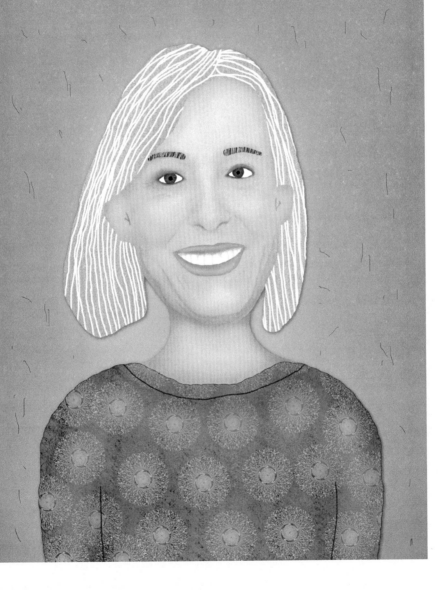

Elizabeth Taylor

Elizabeth Taylor was a very famous English/ American actress, known for her incredible beauty and her many publicized relationships.

She was born in England on 27 February 1932.

Her family were quite well off, and were friends to many famous artists and politicians.

Her family eventually moved to America.

Elizabeth started acting at a very young age, and even from then she was quite popular.

She grew up in the limelight, and said that because of it she did not have much of a childhood.

As Elizabeth matured, she gained more and more leading roles.

She was a very famous actress. Everybody knew her for her beauty, most especially her brilliant eyes.

Elizabeth also received a lot of attention in the media because of her relationships: she got married eight times!

These relationships were sometimes with very famous and rich men.

Elizabeth also did philanthropic work.

She supported charities for HIV/AIDS.

She died on 23 March 2011 from heart failure.

Elizabeth Taylor

Anita Roddick

Anita Roddick was an English business woman, a human rights activist, and a campaigner for the environment.

She was born on 23 October 1942 in England.

She is most well – known for being the founder of The Body Shop.

This cosmetics company was among the first to campaign against the use of animals in the making of their products.

She believed in making natural beauty products that did not harm animals.

The Body Shop was voted the second most trusted brand in the UK.

Anita received criticism when she sold The Body Shop to a much larger corporation.

Anita also supported other charities, including charities for disadvantaged children.

Anita cared very much the rights of human beings and the environment, and dedicate her time to these causes.

She received many awards and honors for the contributions she made to the environment and other charities.

She died on 10 September 2007, at the age of 64.

ANiTA RoddicK

Beatrix Potter

Beatrix Potter was a English writer, most well – known for her famous and well-loved books about Peter Rabbit. She was also a natural scientist and illustrator.

She was born 28 July 1866 in England to wealthy, artistic parents.

She was quite isolated from other children, but she and her brother had many loved pets, and enjoyed drawing.

Even as Beatrix became a scientist, she often drew the specimens she collected.

She and her brother would create their own greeting cards as a way of collecting extra money.

She had the Tale of Peter Rabbit published in 1902, and the stories became very popular.

She also illustrated these stories.

Beatrix was married, but did not have children.

She did a lot to help with the conservation of nature.

Beatrix died on 22 December in 1943.

The Tales of Peter Rabbit are still popular and loved by children all over the world today.

Beatrix Potter

Sappho

Sappho was a Greek poet from the Isle of Lesbos.

Her exact date of birth is not known, but it is estimated at around 630/612 BCE, and her death is recorded to be in 570 BCE.

Not much is known about Sappho.

Most of her biography was pieced together from her poems.

Unfortunately, this does not make for a factual biography!

Sappho was born on the Isle of Lesbos, but due to politics of the time, she was exiled to Sicily.

It is believed that she had a daughter, and that her daughter and mother shared a name.

This was learnt from the poetry that she wrote.

Historians disagree on many aspects of Sappho's life, but it is agreed that Sappho was considered to be one of the greatest Greek poets.

There have also been many recent discoveries of some of Sappho's work, which continues to help historians piece together the story of her life.

There are translations of her Greek poems into English.

SAPPHO

Elizabeth Cady Stanton

Elizabeth Cady Stanton was a respected women's rights activist.

She was born on 12 November 1815 in New York, USA.

Elizabeth came from a very large family – she was one of 11 children!

They grew up in a time when slavery was still legal.

Slavery was only ended a short time after that.

One of the slaves from the Cady family was freed and moved away from the family.

Elizabeth enjoyed going to church with him, and at one point he provided a place for Elizabeth and her sister to stay.

Elizabeth is credited as being amongst the first women to initiate the women's rights movement in America.

Elizabeth fought for many causes within the movement including the right for women to vote, parental rights, rights to divorce, rights to employment and rights to own property!

Elizabeth and her husband had 7 children together.

She died 26 October 1902 at the age of 86.

Elizabeth Cady Stanton

Malala Yousafzai

Malala Yousafzai is the youngest ever winner of a Nobel Prize, winning the Novel Peace Prize for her work in women's rights and the right to education. She was 17 years old.

Malala was born on 12 July 1997 and is 18 years old.

She is from Pakistan.

Malala started defending the rights of women at a young age.

At 11 years old, Malala agreed to do a blog for the BBC regarding the right to education of young girls in Pakistan.

At the time, girls were often banned from attending school.

Malala received many threats on her life for speaking out against terrorism.

She was even shot!

This received worldwide attention.

People were shocked and angered.

Thankfully, Malala made a full recovery.

Malala continues to speak out on the issues of education, and the rights of young women all over the world and especially in her home country, Pakistan.

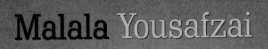

Malala Yousafzai

Betty Williams

Betty Williams is a human rights activist and a Nobel Peace Prize laureate.

Betty was born on 22 May 1943 In Northern Ireland, and is 73 years old.

She received a Nobel Peace prize for the work she did in contributing to peaceful resolutions regarding violent conflicts in Northern Ireland.

Betty worked as a receptionist after completing her education.

She says that her religious background helped her realize that she wanted to be actively involved in peace movements, and helped motivate her to do exactly that.

Betty had witnessed the death of three children after they were struck by a car.

This deeply affected her, and she brought a lot of attention to it to help raise charity.

She believes in anti–violence and often campaigns against violence.

She organised a peace march that was attended by over 10 000 women!

She won the Nobel Peace Prize in 1977.

She is married with children.

Golda Meir

Golda Meir is the 4th Prime Minister of Israel, and she was in office from 1969 to 1974.

She was born on 3 May 1898 in the Russian Empire.

When Golda was young, the family moved from Russia to America.

She was a bright student.

At one point, Golda lived with her sister who often hosted debates and political discussions.

It was here that Golda was exposed to activism.

Golda immigrated to Israel and became involved in politics.

She had a good political career and many positions.

She became Prime Minister on 17 March 1969.

She was described as being a very strong willed and straight forward person and leader.

She was known to be a powerful leader too.

Golda had a husband and together they had two children.

She died on 8 December 1978 at the age of 80.

She is still commemorated to this day for her contributions to Israel's developments.

Golda Meir

Made in the USA
San Bernardino, CA
12 December 2017